ESSENTIAL ELEMENTS

GUITAR SONGS

INCLUDES AUDIO CD

BARRE CHORD ROCK

CONTENTS

ISBN 978-1-4234-3340-8

HAL•LEONARD®
CORPORATION

7777 W. BLUEMOUND RD. P.O. BOX 13819 MILWAUKEE, WI 53213

Visit Hal Leonard Online at
www.halleonard.com

ALL ALONG THE WATCHTOWER

Words and Music by Bob Dylan

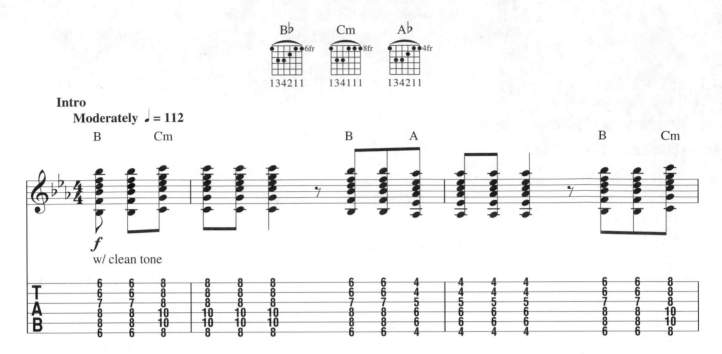

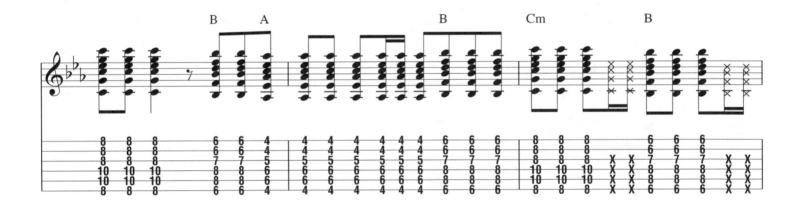

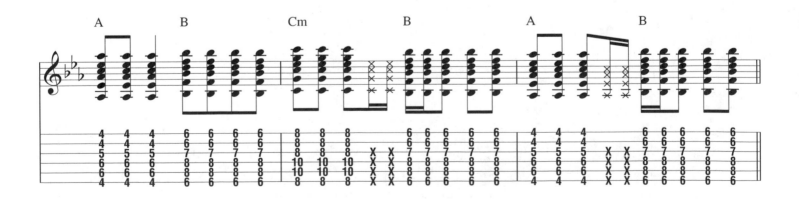

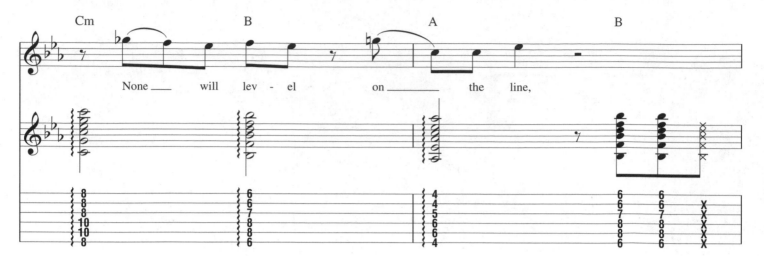

None ___ will lev - el on ___ the line,

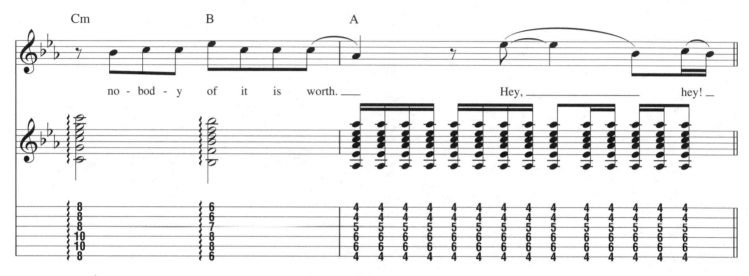

no - bod - y of it is worth. ___ Hey, ___ hey! ___

Guitar Solo

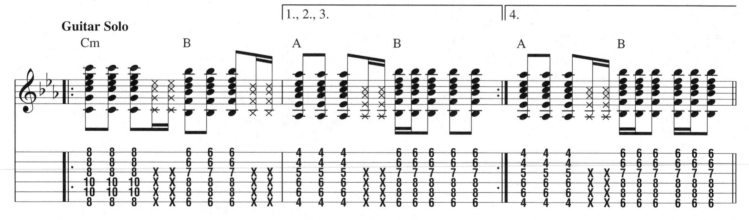

1., 2., 3.   4.

𝄋 **Verse**

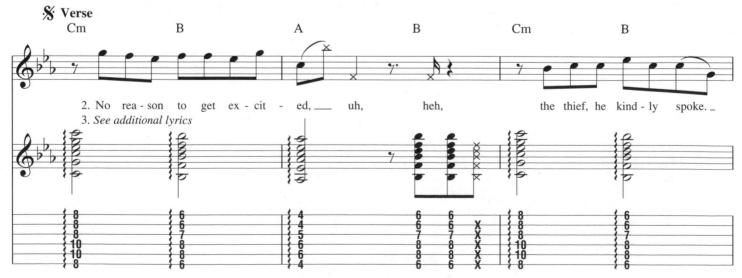

2. No rea - son to get ex - cit - ed, ___ uh, heh, the thief, he kind - ly spoke. ___
3. *See additional lyrics*

6

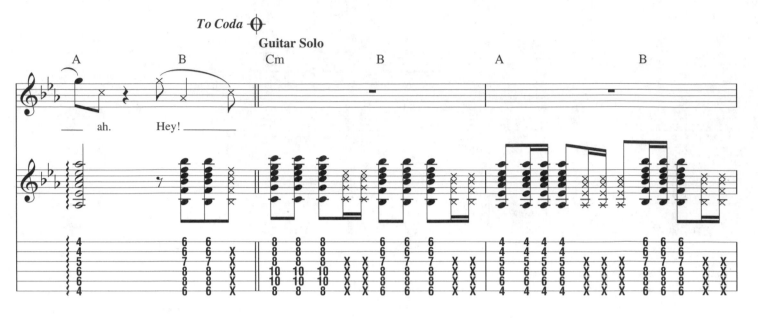

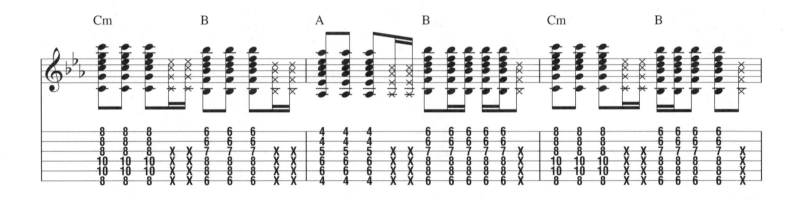

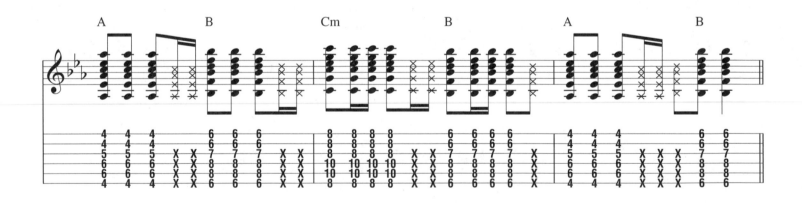

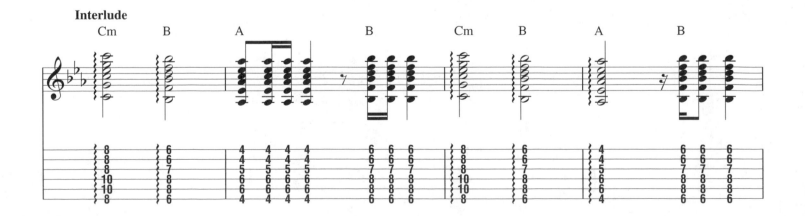

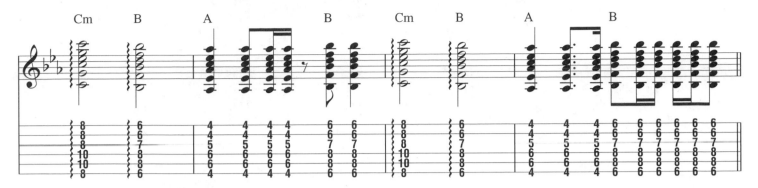

Guitar Solo

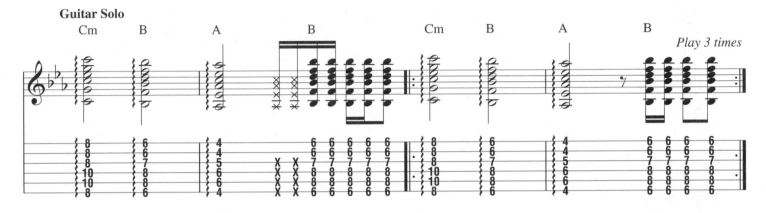

D.S. al Coda

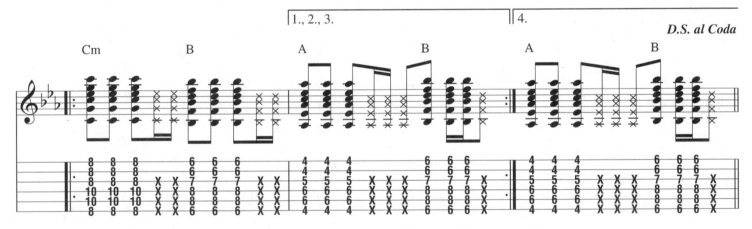

Coda

Outro-Guitar Solo

Repeat and fade

Additional Lyrics

3. All along the watchtower,
   Princes kept the view.
   While all the women came and went,
   Barefoot servants too.
   Well, ah, outside in the cold distance,
   A wild cat did growl.
   Two riders were approachin'
   And the wind began to howl.

BORN TO BE WILD

Words and Music by Mars Bonfire

To Coda

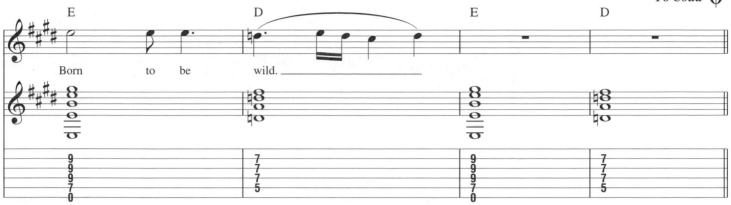

Born to be wild. _____

Organg Solo

Play 3 times

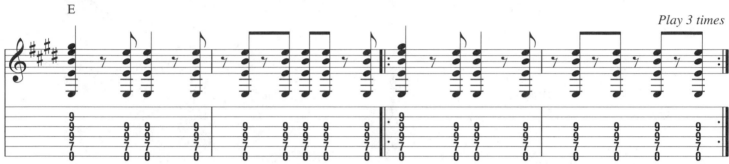

Play 4 times

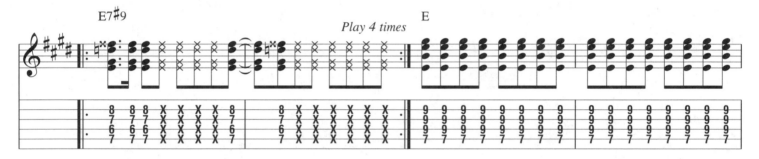

D.S. al Coda

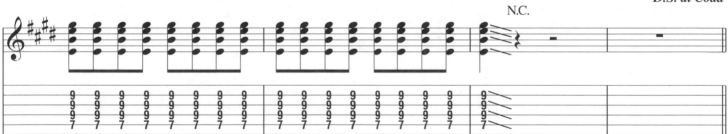

Coda

Outro

Repeat and fade

Play 4 times

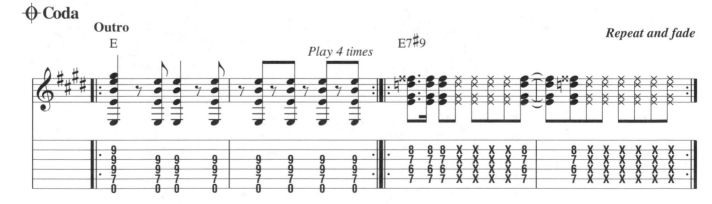

Additional Lyrics

2. I like smoke and lightning,
   Heavy metal thunder,
   Racin' with the wind,
   And the feelin' that I'm under.

I CAN'T EXPLAIN

Words and Music by Peter Townshend

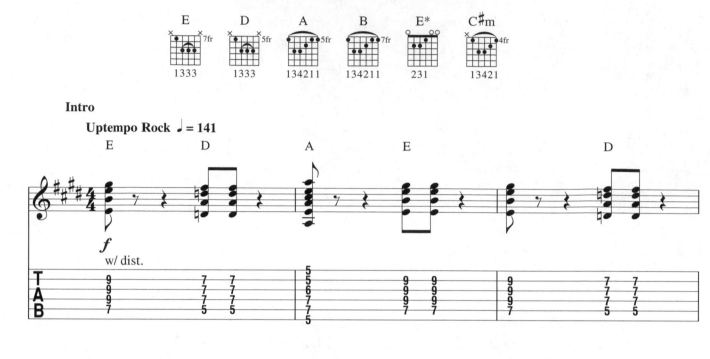

Intro

Uptempo Rock ♩ = 141

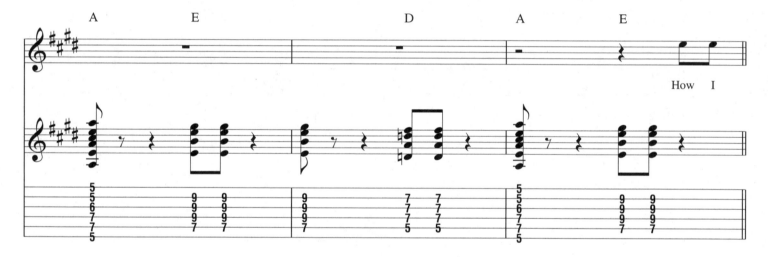

How I

Chorus

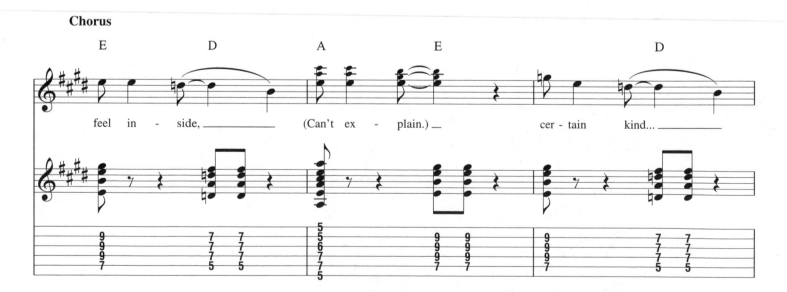

feel in - side, _____ (Can't ex - plain.) _____ cer - tain kind... _____

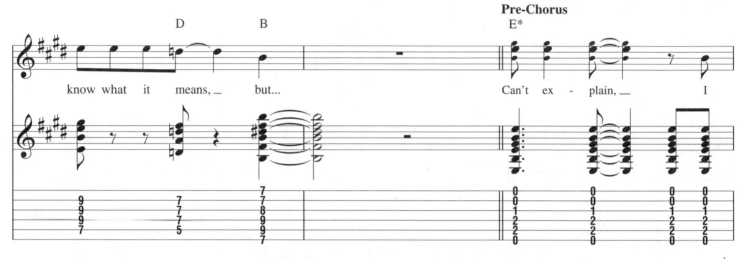

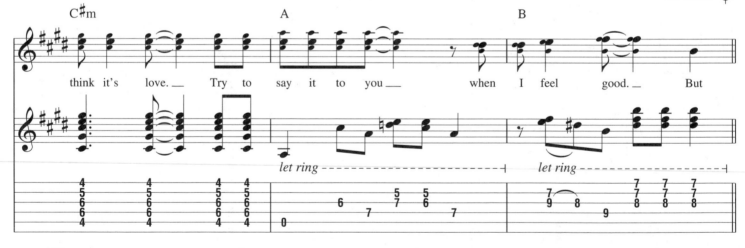

Chorus

Play 4 times

Said, I can't ex - plain __ it.
(Ooh. _____ Can't ex - plain. __

You drive me out of my mind. Tell me
Ooh. _____ Can't ex - plain. __ Ooh. _____

what it's got __ me, yeah. I said I can't ex - plain. __
Can't ex - plain. __ Ooh. _____ Can't ex - plain.) __

Additional Lyrics

2. Dizzy in the head, and I feel bad.
   The things you said got me real mad.
   I'm gettin' funny dreams again and again.
   I know what it means, but...

MELLOW YELLOW

Words and Music by Donovan Leitch

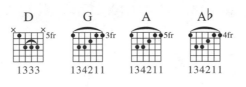

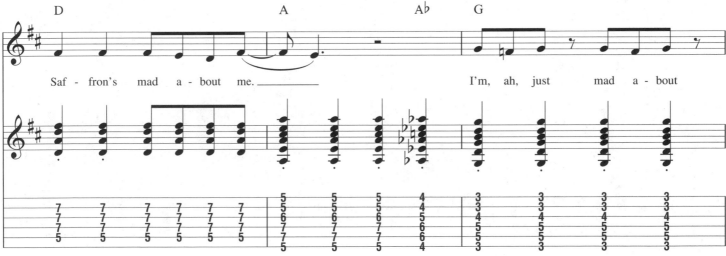

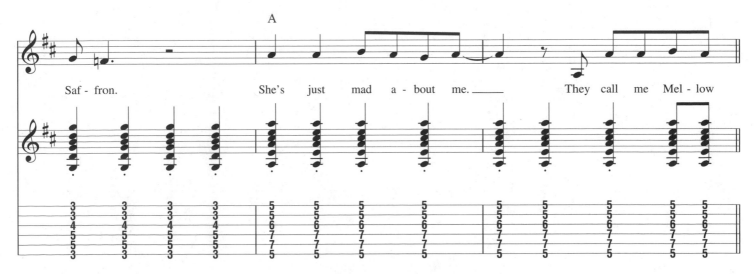

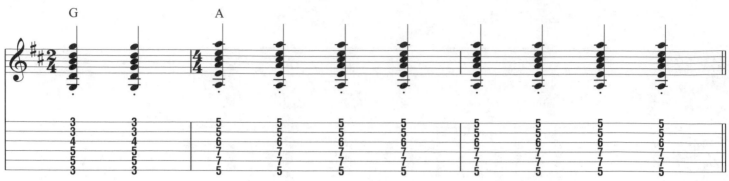

Verse

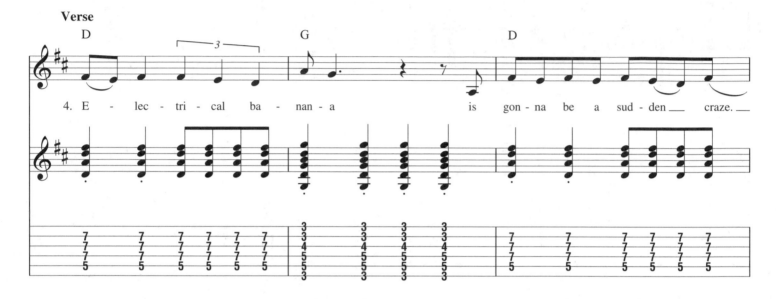

4. E - lec - tri - cal ba - nan - a   is gon - na be a sud - den ___ craze. ___

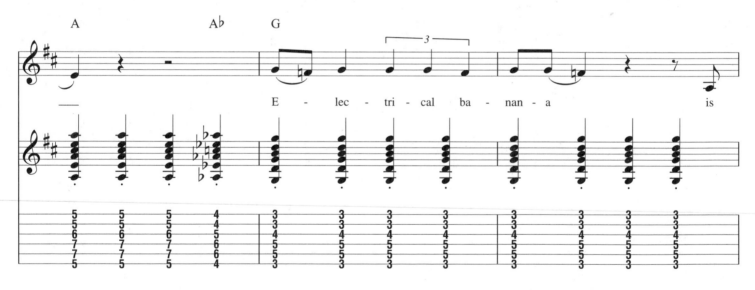

___ E - lec - tri - cal ba - nan - a   is

Chorus

bound to be the ver - y next phase. ___ They call it Mel - low Yel - low. ___

They call me Mel - low Yel - low. _____ They call me Mel - low

Yel - low. _____ 5. Eh, ___

Verse

_____ Saf - fron. Yeah. ___ I'm just mad a - bout her. ___

_____ Well, I'm, buh, just, uh, mad a - bout, uh, Saf - fron.

Outro-Chorus

She's just mad a-bout me. ____ They call me Mel - low Yel - low. ____

They call me Mel - low Yel - low. ____ Oh, so ____

____ yel - low. ____ Oh, ____ so mel - low. ____

Oh, so mel - low. ____

Begin fade

Fade out

NOWHERE MAN

Words and Music by John Lennon and Paul McCartney

Chorus

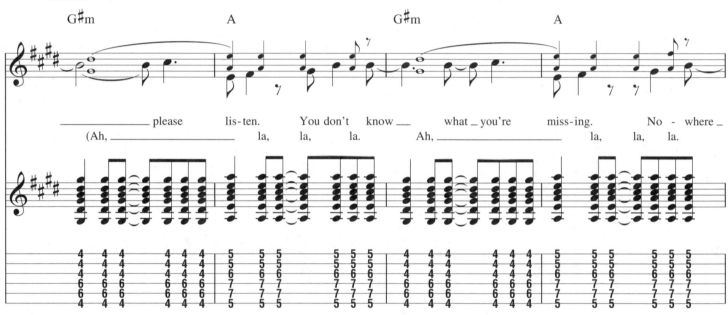

To Coda ⊕

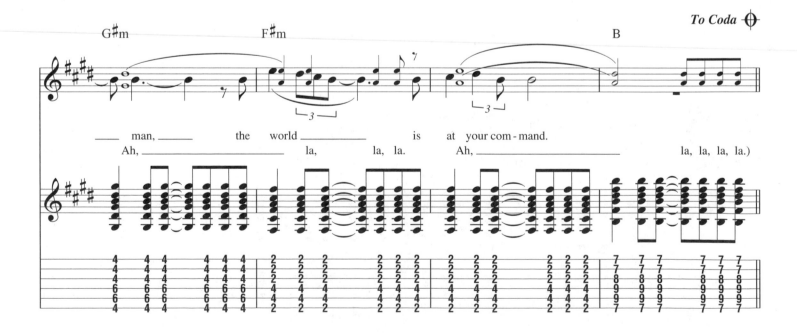

Guitar Solo

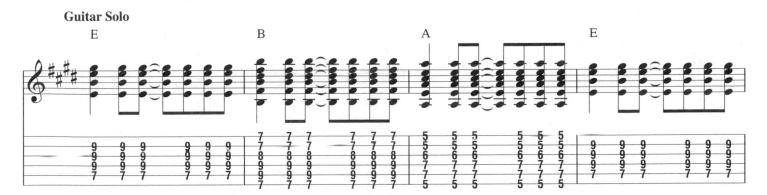

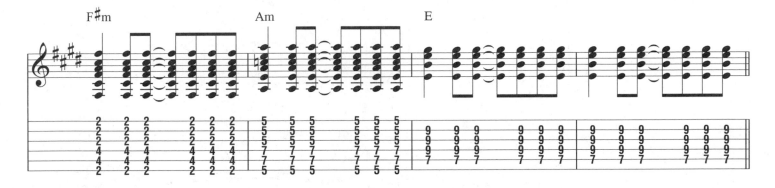

Verse

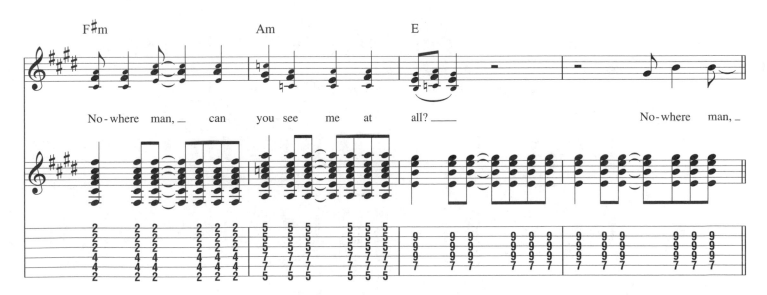

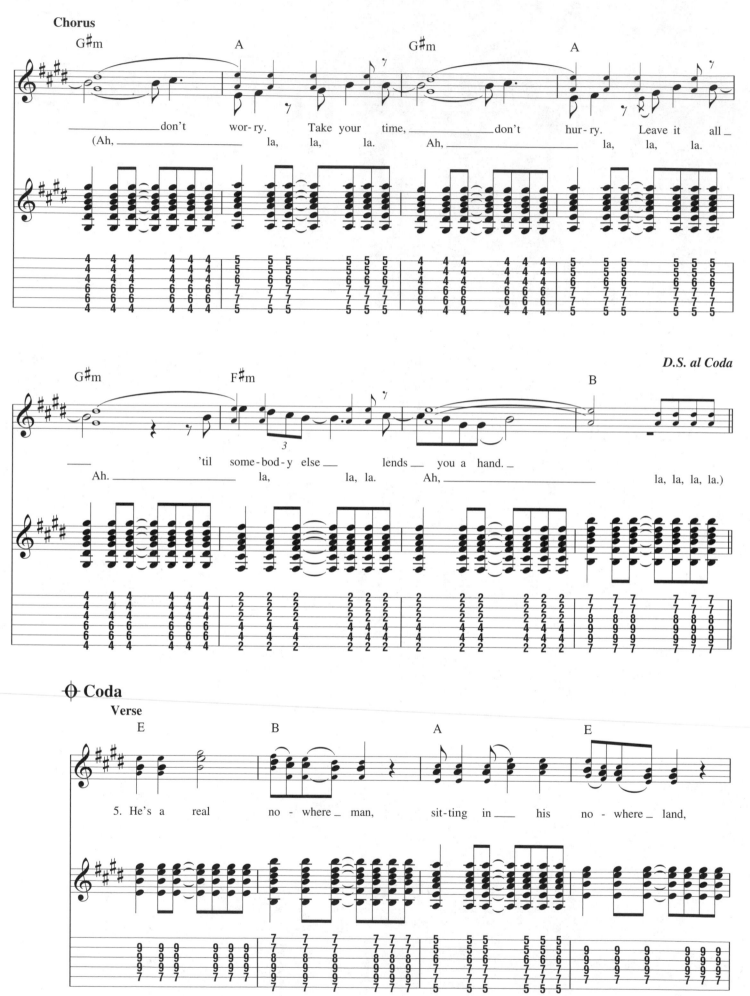

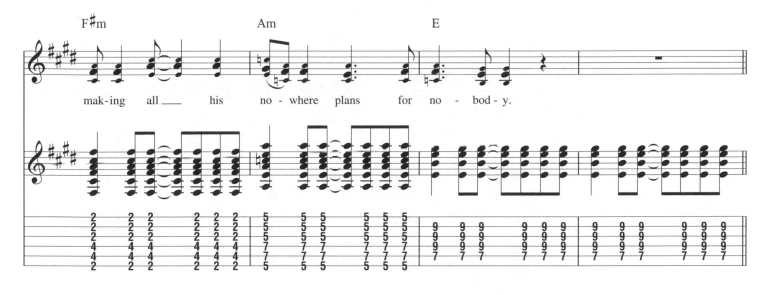

Outro

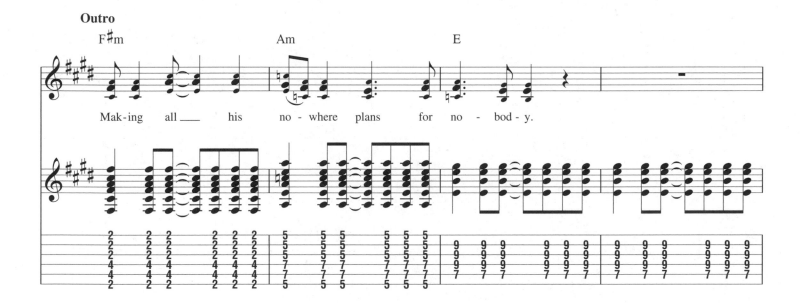

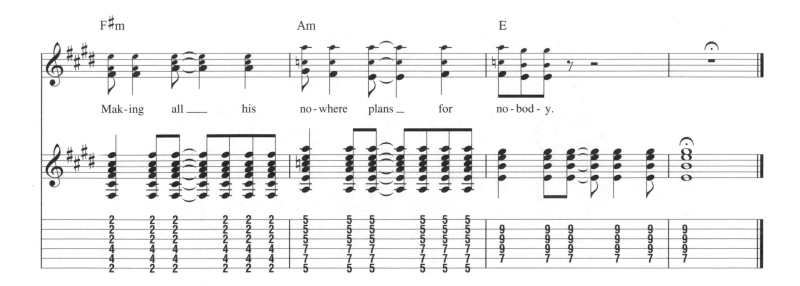

STRAY CAT STRUT

Words and Music by Brian Setzer

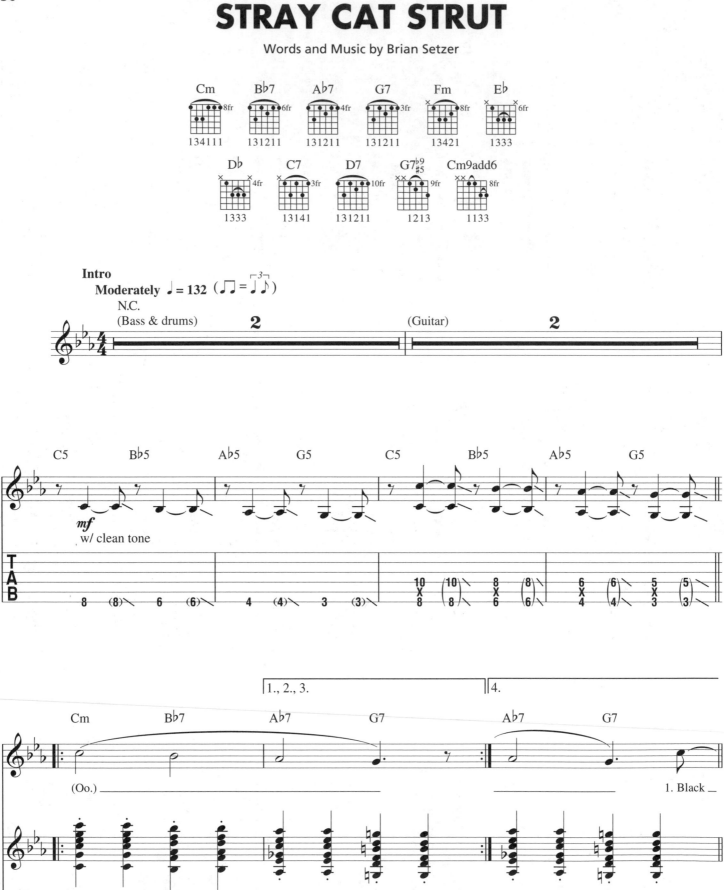

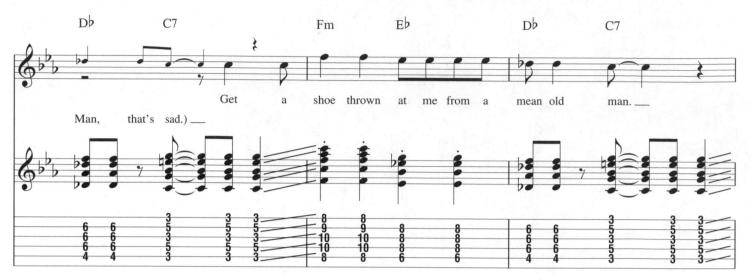

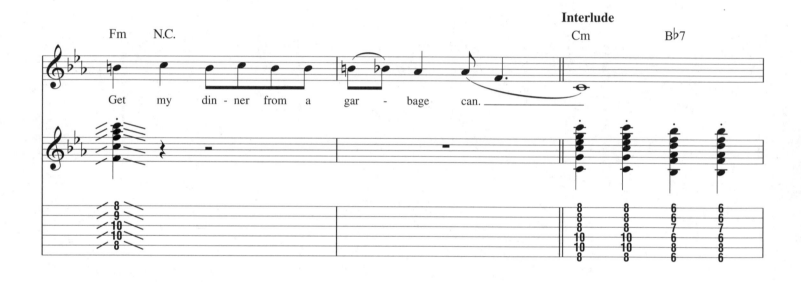

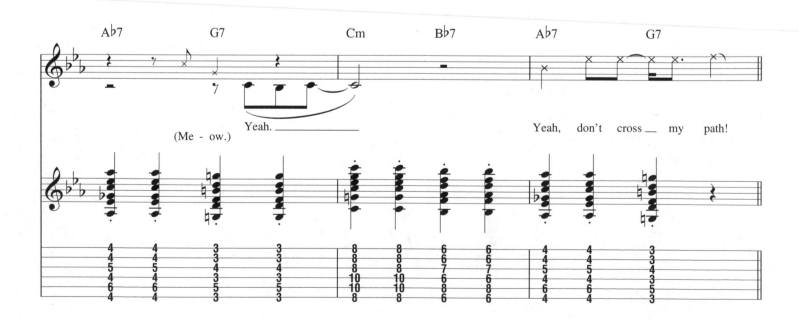

Guitar Solo

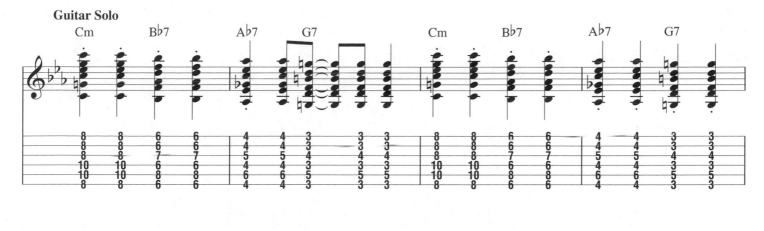

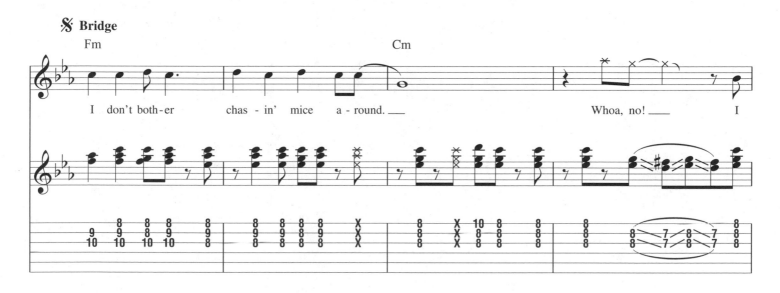

𝄋 Bridge

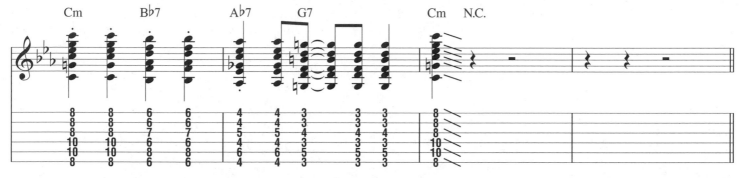

I don't both-er chas-in' mice a-round. ___ Whoa, no! ___ I

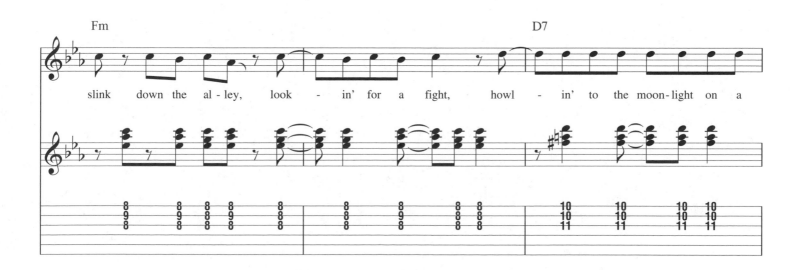

slink down the al-ley, look-in' for a fight, howl-in' to the moon-light on a

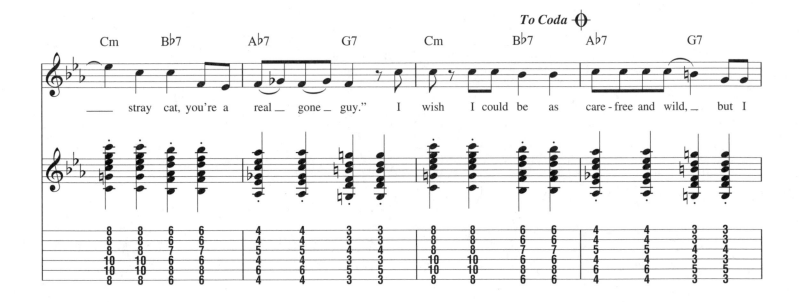

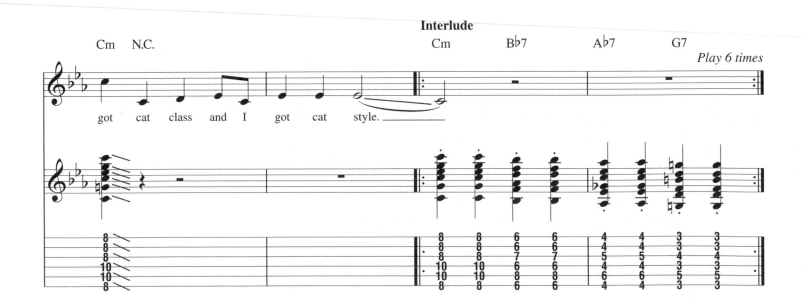

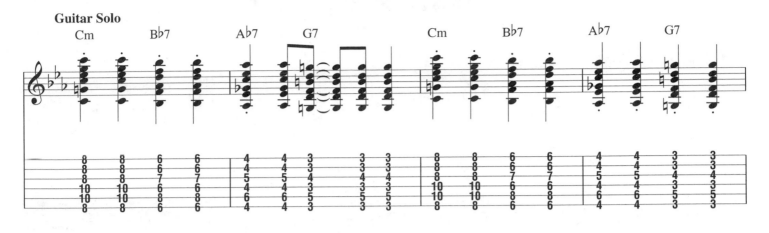

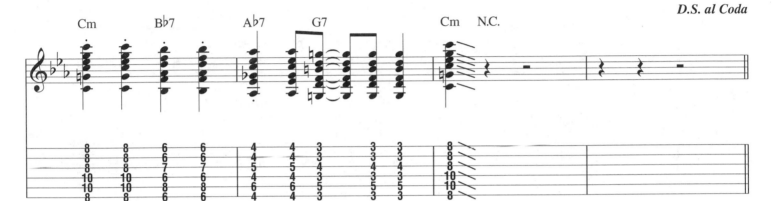

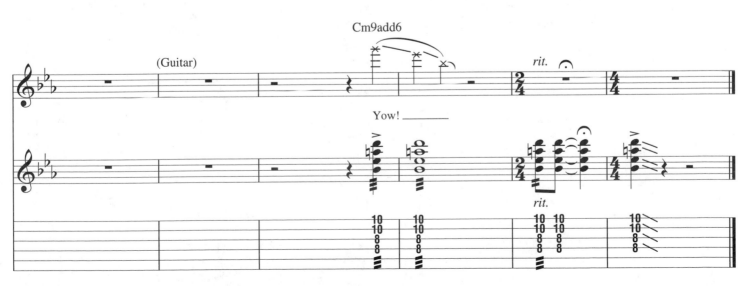

SUMMER OF '69

Words and Music by Bryan Adams and Jim Vallance

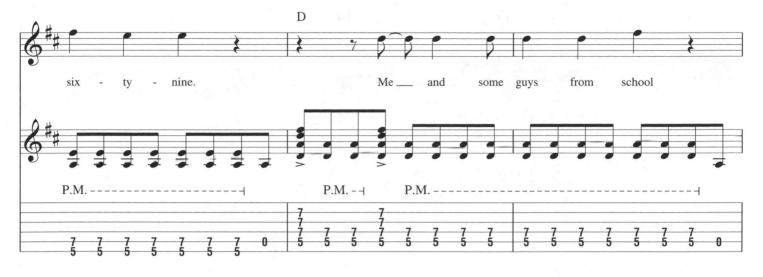

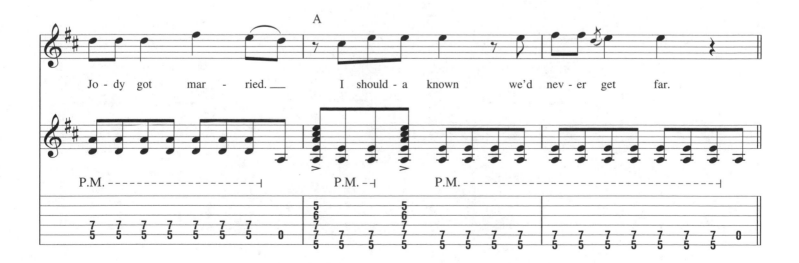

%: Pre-Chorus

1. Oh, when I look back now, ___ that sum - mer seemed to
2., 3. *See additional lyrics*

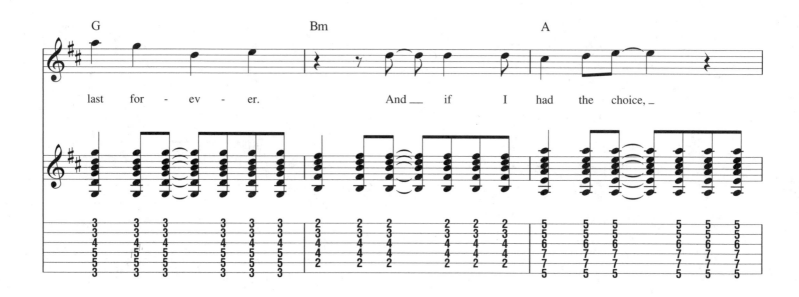

last for - ev - er. And ___ if I had the choice, ___

yeah, ___ I'd al - ways wan - na be there. Those ___ were the

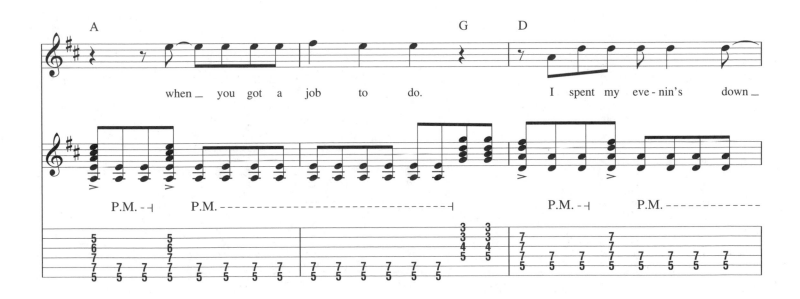

D.S. al Coda 1

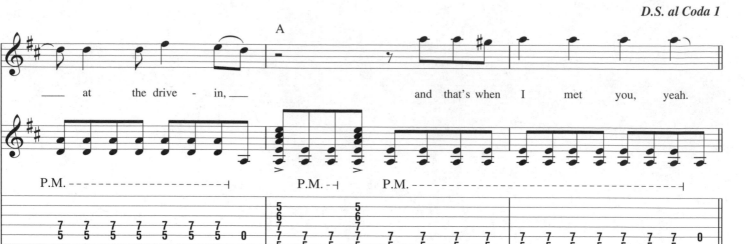

at the drive - in, ___ and that's when I met you, yeah.

P.M. - - - - - - - - - - - - - - - - P.M. - - P.M. - - - - - - - - - - - - - - - - - -

Coda 1

Chorus

life. Oh, ___ yeah. ___

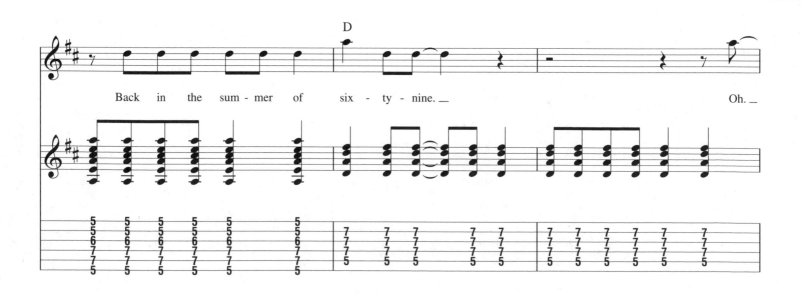

Back in the sum - mer of six - ty - nine. ___ Oh. ___

Verse

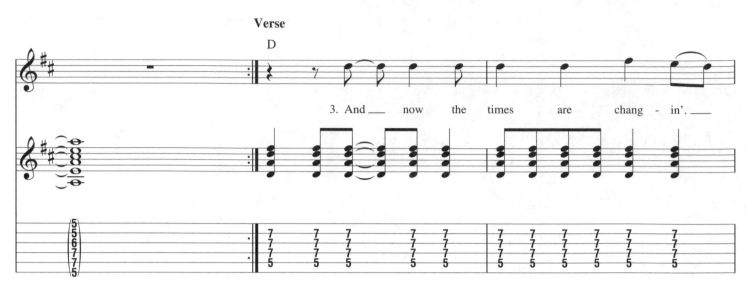

3. And ___ now the times are chang - in'. ___

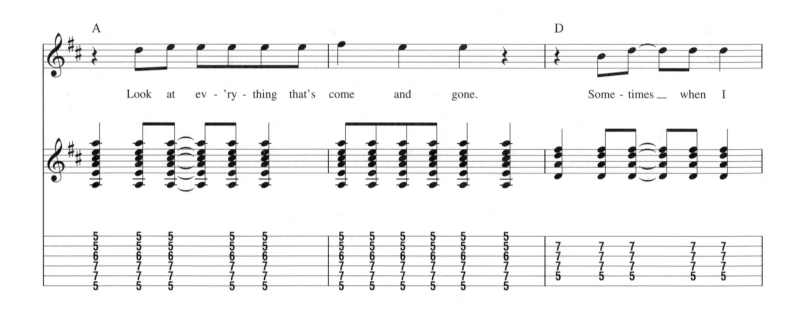

Look at ev - 'ry - thing that's come and gone. Some - times ___ when I

D.S. al Coda 2

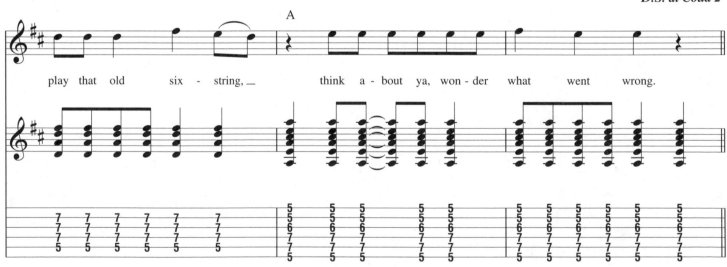

play that old six - string, ___ think a - bout ya, won - der what went wrong.

Coda 2

life.

Oh, _____ yeah. ___

Outro

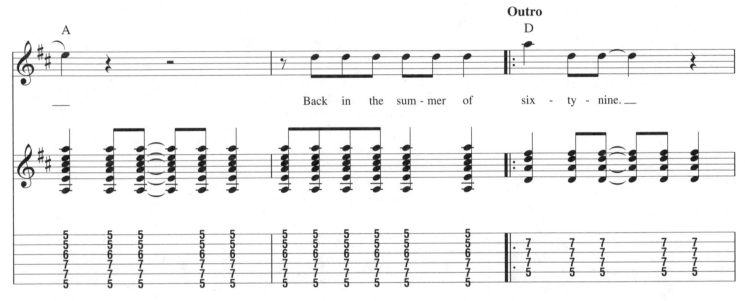

___

Back in the sum-mer of six-ty-nine. ___

Repeat and fade

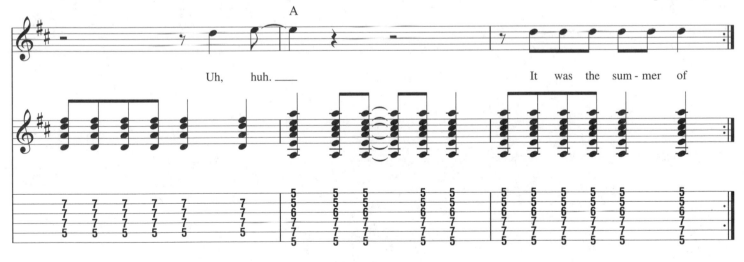

Uh, huh. ___

It was the sum-mer of

Additional Lyrics

Pre-Chorus 2., 3. Standin' on your mama's porch

You told me that { you'd wait / it'd last } forever.

Oh, and when you held my hand,
I knew that it was now or never.
Those were the best days of my life.

WILD THING

Words and Music by Chip Taylor

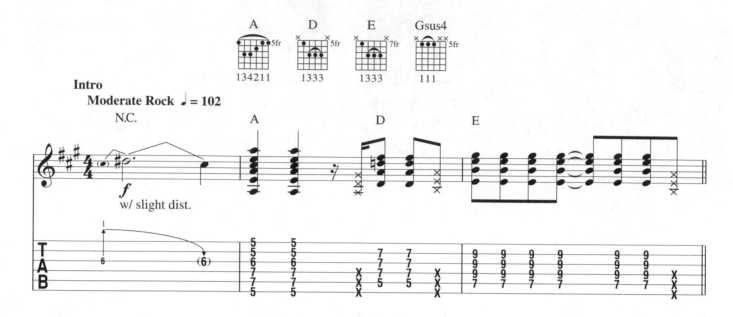

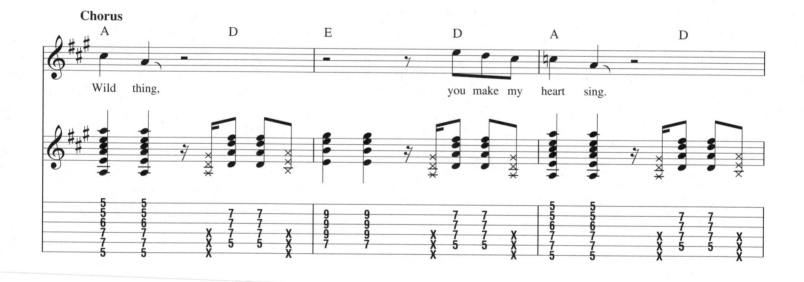

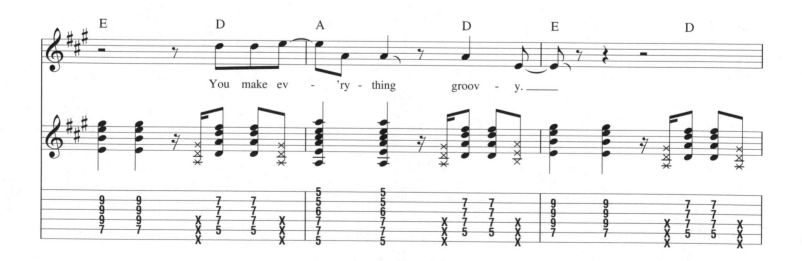

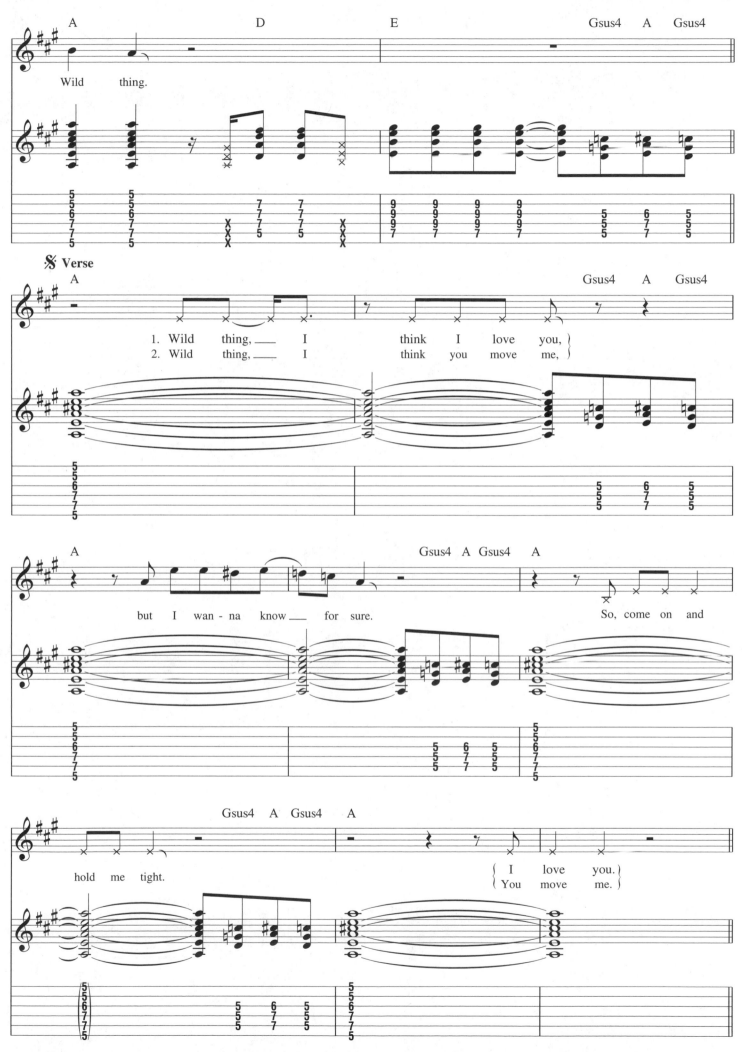

To Coda ⊕

Pre-Chorus

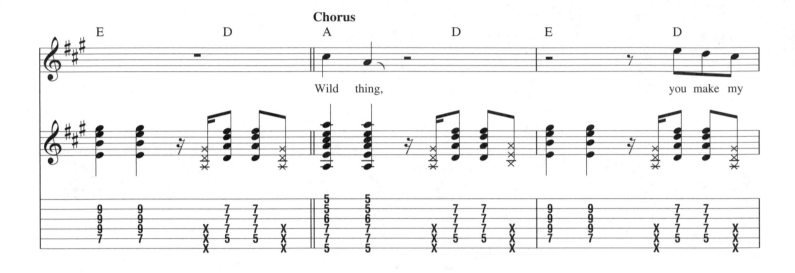

Chorus

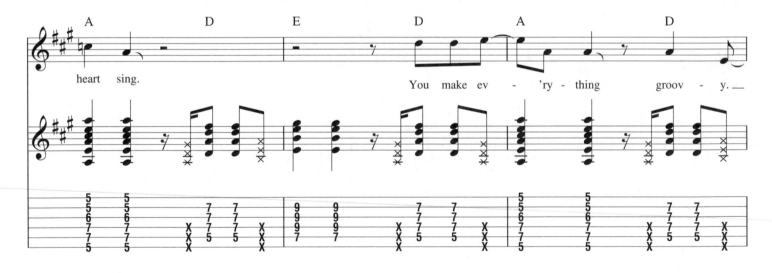

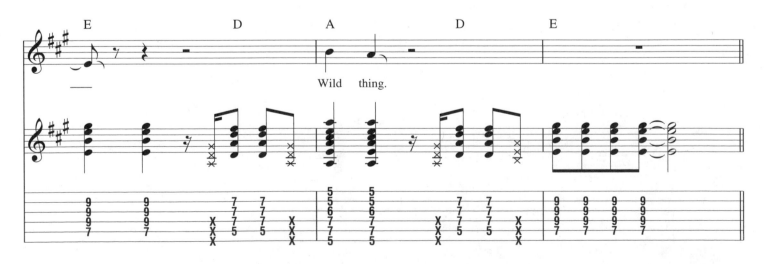

Recorder Solo

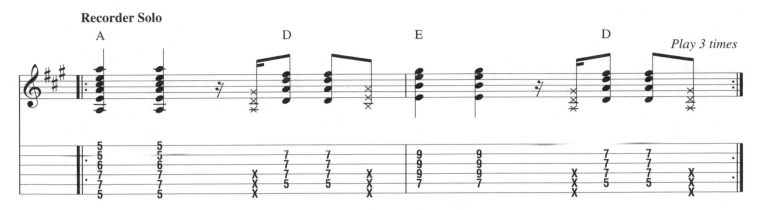

D.S. al Coda

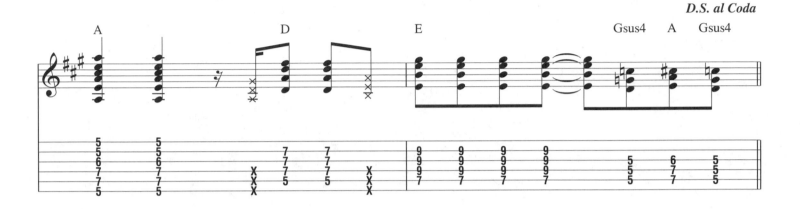

Coda

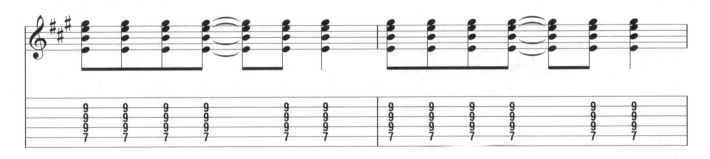

Outro-Chorus

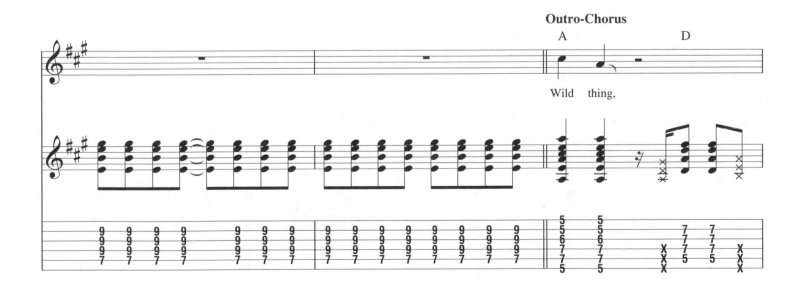

Wild   thing,

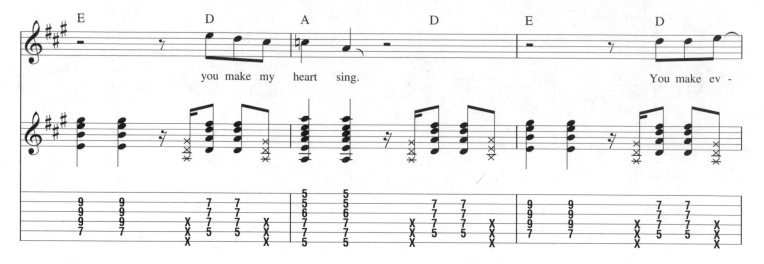

you make my heart sing. You make ev -

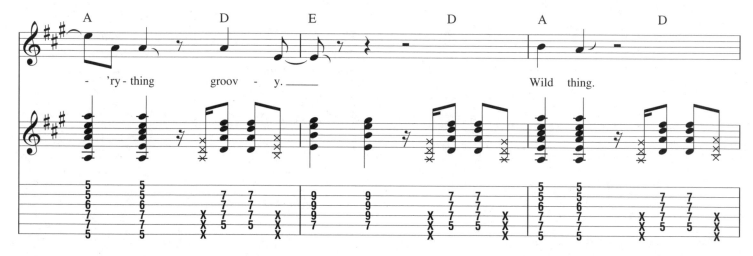

- 'ry - thing groov - y. _____ Wild thing.

Begin fade

Come on, ___ come on, wild thing. Shake it, ___ shake it,

Fade out

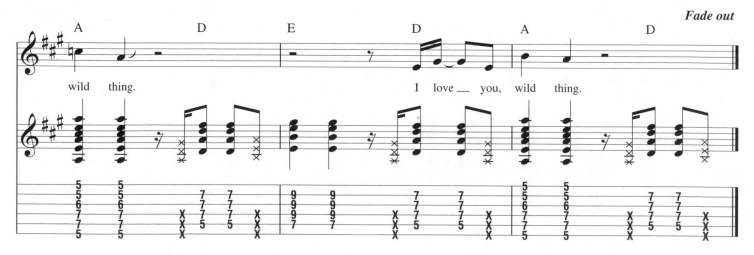

wild thing. I love ___ you, wild thing.